Crystal Bailey
28 Kensington Close
Spruce Grove, AB
T7X 0S9
780-913-2009

This Journal Belongs to:

Name ....

Email ....

Telephone ....

Breathe

Balance

JOURNAL

STERLING
New York

Balance

Do you jump out of bed each morning raring to go? Do you often feel excited about the day ahead? What about inspired and full of ideas? Answer no to any of these questions and some will say you're in the wrong job, or you haven't yet found your true calling. But even if you're doing what you love, it's easy to get sucked into a spiral of doing more and more of the less essential things.

Pausing to take stock and reprioritize the vital elements of your life can create a more balanced way to live and have a positive effect on overall well-being. Reprioritizing will mean different things for different people, but for most it's about focusing on the biggest joys in life and making changes to bring them to the fore.

And that's where this journal can help. Think of it as your chance to take a step back, make time for your thoughts, feelings, and physical self, and discover what's really important. What makes you happy? What do you love to do more than anything? What makes you feel relaxed, physically and mentally? It's time to shift the balance and find your equilibrium.

Contents

Accentuate the Positive

Can having a more optimistic outlook actually affect what happens in your life? Even if you're a pessimist, taking a more balanced view of situations could make you happier.

Maybe you're a glass half-full kind of person. Or you might be quite the opposite—a born pessimist, prone to imagining the worst possible outcomes. Or maybe, like many people, you swing between the two, depending on your feelings and the current situation. While some might be happy to identify themselves as one or the other, for others it isn't quite so cut and dried. Whatever your perspective, there can be something quite attractive about an optimistic outlook: seeing the good in things, looking for the bright side, and spotting the positives.

The Secret to Happiness?

Tali Sharot, a professor of cognitive neuroscience at University College London, believes that optimists generally report having a happier life. In a 2012 TED Talk, she talks about how eighty percent of the population are hardwired toward an optimistic bias. Ask these idealists how likely it is that their marriage will work out, for instance, and they'll tell you that it's a dead certainty, despite soaring divorce rates. There are plenty of other, similar examples, all pointing to the fact that people within this majority view their own talents, family, and futures with a generally positive slant. While they might not apply this rose-tinted view to the rest of the world, or even their neighbor, they have faith that their private world is going to be okay because they choose to believe it will.

Self-Fulfilling Prophecy

Tali claims that those who experience mild depression have an arguably more realistic outlook, while those on the more severe end of the spectrum tend toward a pessimistic bias. But while a realistic view of the world might help soften the blow of disappointment, divorce, or job loss, it's positive thinking that can help set you up for success.

"Optimism changes subjective reality," she says. "The way we expect the world to be alters the way we see it. But it also changes objective reality—it acts as a self-fulfilling prophecy. Lowering your expectations will not make you happy. Controlled experiments have shown that optimism is not only related to success, it also leads to it . . . in academia, sports, and politics. And maybe the most surprising benefit of a positive outlook is health. If we expect the future to be promising, stress and anxiety are reduced."

Train Your Brain

So, if looking on the bright side can lead to a happier, healthier life, where does that leave those who naturally tend toward a less-than-sunny disposition? Is it possible to learn optimism? The answer appears to be a resounding yes. According to Dr. Alex Lickerman—a physician, former director of primary care at the University of Chicago, and practicing Buddhist—what you tell yourself will play a large part in how you feel about yourself, your abilities, and the rest of the world. He gives the example of failing a test. If you see it through a pessimistic view, telling yourself you're simply no good at exams, it becomes a self-fulfilling prophecy and you're more likely to go into future tests preparing to do badly. But if you adopt a more positive outlook, for example telling yourself you could have studied harder, then you take back control of the situation. You could redouble your efforts, study harder, and pass on the second go.

Keep One Foot in Reality

Dr. Lickerman, author of *The Ten Worlds* and *The Undefeated Mind*, explains that this rosy perspective doesn't have to be at the expense of actualities. "Realistic optimists don't blithely assume they can accomplish anything or overcome any obstacle. They recognize the need for real effort but feel motivated, not inhibited, by their worry that they might not achieve their goals." Talking about these two viewpoints of the world and of the self, Dr. Lickerman continues, "Like any other personality characteristic, how optimistic or pessimistic we are is largely influenced by our genes and, to a lesser degree, by our experiences.

"People with a pessimistic self-explanatory style are at greater risk of becoming depressed and committing suicide [*sic*] when adversity strikes. On the other hand, being too optimistic can blind you to the need to make efforts to accomplish your goals and can lead to complacency." Though thought processes are influenced by genetics and environmental factors, Alex believes it's still possible to train the brain to change its go-to response, especially when that response is negative and does you no favors.

Challenge Your Response

Dr. Lickerman refers to a study that had subjects looking for alternative explanations for the causes of life events. He says, "The mere act of not settling for the first explanation you find for an event ['I failed the test because I'm stupid'] but challenging yourself to look for alternative explanations ['Maybe I failed because I really didn't study hard enough'] tends to naturally lead to more optimistic explanations." Challenging that first, knee-jerk response to a situation works. It takes time and patience, but it appears that with practice and a commitment to challenge established neural patterns, the switch can be made.

Optimism has its benefits, a realistic version even more so. But if you're the person who's never going to be like that, that's fine too. There's no one-size-fits-all approach to life and handling the ups and downs of living. Perhaps cynicism has helped you avoid situations that have tripped up more trusting folk. Maybe being on your guard has kept you safe and away from people who drain your energy and time. In the words of novelist Jean Rhys, "We can't all be happy, we can't all be rich, we can't all be lucky—and it would be so much less fun if we were. There must be the dark background to show up the bright colors."

SIX STEPS TO OPTIMISM

1. Look for Another View

If you always react in a certain way, now might be a good time to challenge that train of thought.

Stop and ask yourself if there's another point from which you could view a situation that you have a negative viewpoint about. Write down the opposite, more optimistic response here. How does thinking in this way make you feel?

....

....

....

....

....

....

2. Be a Copycat

If it doesn't feel natural to speak optimistically, mimic someone who does. Use some of their turns of phrase and see if saying them makes you feel more positive.

List a few optimists in your life that you'd like to mimic. Write down some of their expressions here and refer back to them when you're in need of a quick dose of positivity.

....

....

....

....

....

....

3. Use Affirmations

It's easy to internalize failure into pessimism, but saying positive mantras aloud to yourself in difficult situations can make you feel better and spur you onward.

You can say things like:

- *I am loved.*
- *I am strong and successful.*
- *I don't sweat the small stuff.*
- *I am confident in my ability to. . . .*
- *I give myself space to grow and learn.*
- *I trust that I am on the right path.*

Use this space to jot down some specific affirmations that resonate with you.

....

....

....

....

....

....

4. Focus on Past Success

While it's easy to see your failures, try to bring to mind times in your life when you've had real successes.

Jot them down here, focusing particularly on how you felt.

....

....

....

....

....

....

5. Live in the Moment

When you imagine that everything's going to go wrong, so often it can and will. Staying present and making the best of things now can take stress and worry out of the future and brighten your mood.

If you notice yourself starting to catastrophize, use the following meditation to bring yourself back to the present moment:

• Adopt a comfortable posture but not one in which you are likely to fall asleep. Sitting upright is more effective than lying down.

• Set up your mind's gatekeeper, whose job is to control what comes in and what stays out. Be clear of their role at the outset—silently repeat the following three times: "Now is the time to be aware of the present moment. I let go of the past and the future."

• Turn your attention to any sounds in your environment. First focus on obvious ones and as your concentration gets sharper, notice subtler sounds, such as bird calls and distant chatter or traffic. Allow them to wash over you, letting go of the sounds that have passed by and being present to new ones as they arise.

• Feel all your bodily sensations—your arms resting on your lap, your legs on the chair, your clothes against your skin. Notice any pains, tightness, or anxious feelings. Watch how these sensations shift and change, letting go of them and becoming present to those that arise.

• Watch your thoughts arise and pass, without getting caught up or feeling that you have to act on them. Some are nonsense; others you might follow. Observe demanding thoughts, label them, and let them go. For example, if you are thinking, "I'm upset over that insult," you might label it "hurt" and let it go so that you're ready for the next thought to arise. It's like watching clouds passing in the sky. You are aiming for a "blue sky mind" where storm clouds pass and the mind is clear, calm, and alert.

• Watch the natural changes in your breathing as you become calmer. You might notice that your breath starts shallow and fast, but becomes deeper and more regular as you relax.

6. An Attitude of Gratitude

So often does the bad overshadow the good, but if you write down all the good things in your life, you'll start seeing so much more positivity. Feeling thankful will help you feel more optimistic about the future and the good things that are in store for you.

What are you grateful for? Write it down here.

Rest Stop

Few question that exercise is beneficial for the body and mind, but at a time when many follow a more-is-more philosophy and work out every day, it's easy to neglect the need for balance and give yourself enough recovery time from the exertion.

Sometimes, exercise is a struggle. In other moments, it feels so easy—be it going for a run or slotting in an extra power yoga class—that you don't feel complete without the workout fix. And there's no doubt that it's beneficial. Physical activity improves muscle strength and stamina, supports cardiovascular health, and aids mental well-being. As the mental health organization Mind points out, exercising can bring better sleep and help manage stress, anxiety, and depression. But it's important not to lose sight of the other side of the exercise coin: rest. Rest days—or even longer periods—are an important part of the process required to build strength, endurance, and muscle.

Less Is More
Hollie Grant, instructor and founder of Pilates PT, says people overlook rest at their peril. "Some of the most common signs that someone is overtraining are injury, a reduction in results, and lethargy," she says. "None of these is desirable, and they [often] come from a lack of appropriate rest between training sessions." She adds that many poor workouts is not equivalent to fewer good-quality ones. "Sadly, the 'more-is-more' mentality is rife. We see fitness influencers exercising every day online, and we can [therefore] understandably believe this is normal, but we do need rest." Overdoing the stress on the body can lead to overuse injuries, such as stress fractures, muscle strains, and joint pain.

Work Out Well

When you exercise, whether it's by running, strength training, or interval sessions, tiny tears are created in the muscles. In the process of repairing the muscles, they grow stronger, so the same workout can be performed with less effort next time. But if they're not given time between sessions to mend, the tears can lead to sprains or tendon injuries such as tendonitis—inflammation caused by overuse. The time needed to repair depends on age, fitness level, and genes, plus the intensity and length of the workouts. Rest days give muscles the chance to grow. They're necessary for avoiding exercise-induced fatigue and reduce the chance of injury.

Physical activity also depletes the muscles' store of glycogen levels, which need time to be replaced to prevent soreness and tiredness. Bones also benefit from down days, something that's especially important for runners, whose legs absorb the shock of the surface on which they're running. Even the fittest and most resilient athletes are advised to take at least one day off during their working week, which suggests that it's vital that we all factor in down periods and recovery as part of our exercise program.

Find the Right Mix For You

"Rest improves performance, increases results, and reduces risk of injury," says Hollie. "If you must do something every day—and I would suggest asking yourself why you feel the need to—then ensure you mix it up." She says nobody should be practicing high-intensity interval training (HIIT) every day. "It takes the body around forty-eight hours to replace glycogen stores after a HIIT workout, so doing another similar session within that time will mean there's less energy in the tank." Instead, she suggests doing a low-intensity activity, such as Pilates or yoga, and returning to HIIT when the body is ready. "Rest is the most important part of your fitness regime, and without it you will struggle to get the results you want." She adds that missing it might also strip the fun out of activities you usually enjoy and turn the exercise you love into a chore.

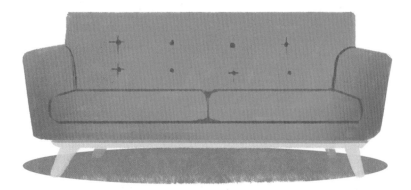

Body and Mind

Rest not only gives the body time to repair and strengthen itself between workouts but also provides the mind space to reset psychologically and can help to maintain motivation. Immediate or short-term recovery usually occurs within hours after an exercise session or event, and includes low-intensity activity after working out and during the cool-down phase, while long-term recovery refers to specific periods built into a seasonal training schedule and might last days or weeks. Elite athletes are drilled in the importance of rest as part of their training. While many rise early, have punishing schedules, and aren't afraid to push themselves in the gym or on the track or the court, they also understand the value of pressing pause and value well-deserved TLC.

Active Rest

Not all take a full day off to rest, however. Some might have an active rest or recovery day, where they keep the body moving with low-intensity workouts that encourage muscle repair without too much strain. This might include a Pilates class, which is excellent for injury prevention and body awareness; foam rolling, which helps with deep-tissue or myofascial release; or gentle forms of yoga. Paul Sullivan teaches these gentle forms, such as yin and restorative, alongside more dynamic, powerful, and sports variants. He points out that ashtanga advocates, for example, practice for six days a week, taking rest on Saturdays and the days of the new and full Moon. "It's vital to honor your body by allowing a day of rest from the physical," he says. "Recharging, rejuvenating, and reconnecting are all powerful ways to create your own inner awareness and quality of life." Paul incorporates the three Bs—breath (pranayama), body awareness, and balance. "Rest days are essential in supporting a busy lifestyle, as they create a space when we can truly honor our physical selves and allow gentle or thoughtful practices such as hatha, yin, or restorative yoga to help create inner awareness." He also suggests meditation or pausing and turning inward to be fully present.

Importance of Zs

Integral to good rest, of course, is good sleep, which is a vital recovery and performance enhancer. Many athletes consider it to be just what their muscles need to rest and recover from strenuous daily training. Retired Jamaican sprinter Usain Bolt, who won twenty Olympic and world championship gold medals between 2008 and 2016, says he sleeps between eight and ten hours a night. "It's extremely important to me. I need to rest and recover in order for the training I do to be absorbed by my body." Scotland's tennis champion Andy Murray, winner of three Grand Slams, has also commented on sleep. At the time of his 2013 Wimbledon win, he enjoyed around twelve hours shut-eye a night. "Rest is so important. You need it to make sure you recover properly."

"Take rest; a field that has rested gives a bountiful crop."

Ovid

Immune Boost

Rest days will also support your immune system. A study published in the *European Journal of Sport Science*, which focuses on athletes but includes advice that is relevant for everyone, points out that while modern exercise reduces the risk of colds and flu, bouts of long, hard, and intense training can leave a person prone to upper respiration tract infections. This is partly caused by increased levels of stress hormones that suppress white blood-cell functions, leaving the athlete open to infection. What is the right balance? There's no magic number of rest days because you have to factor in fitness, genes, intensity of workouts, and general stress levels in your life. But listening to your body and making note of your level of tiredness and muscle sorenesss will help you work out what's appropriate for you. And if Usain Bolt says sleep is good for you, then try to complement it with lots of Zs too.

DO YOU NEED TO GIVE IT A REST?

As a general guideline, if you're not used to lots of exercise you might need to take two or three rest days per week, while one day might be enough for those with more experience. If you're trying to decide whether you need more recovery time in your schedule, ask yourself the following questions, noting your answers over the course of a week or two to see any patterns emerging.

Am I exhausted before I even start exercising?

....

....

....

....

....

....

Am I feeling new aches and pains throughout my week?

....

....

....

....

....

....

....

Am I experiencing a burned-out feeling, either physically or mentally?

....

....

....

....

....

....

Am I relying on caffeine or energy drinks to get through my days?

....

....

....

....

....

....

If you've answered yes to any of these questions, it's worth considering taking a break from your workout routine and investing more time in caring for your physical and mental well-being. When planning your recovery day, consider what makes you feel rested—that is, revived, refreshed, and renewed. The sense of reaching a restored feeling could come from a gentle walk outdoors, an hour or so tucked up on the couch with a book, meditation, mindfulness practice, or breathing exercises.

Body Language

Different moods bring about different physical manifestations and perspectives, but it's possible to exercise more control and balance over them.

Surprise tugs eyebrows into high arches, anger balls up fists, and pride thrusts out chests—reactions and emotions are embodied. They reflect the nuances of experience and sculpt them into universally recognizable shapes. According to Richard Bandler and John Grinder—creators of neurolinguistic programming (NLP), a discipline that assumes there's a link between neurological processes, language, and behavior—how we are in any given moment depends on focus, physiology, and self-talk.

Changing what you're picturing in your head, the way you're holding your body, or what you're saying to yourself can alter your perspective. An NLP premise is that a state only lasts for 90 seconds before it needs to be "refilled" with whatever triggered it in the first place. If delight, disgust, or daring linger, it means they are being continuously fired off. It's helpful to recognize the cause, take appropriate action, and then make adjustments. While people don't have complete control over their moods, they can influence them, and moving is one way to achieve this.

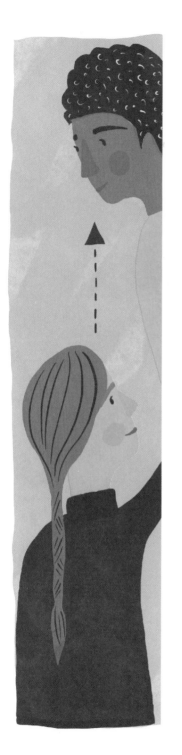

Positive Postures

Physical experience is encoded in a person's emotional vocabulary: "I'm feeling down," "I look up to him/her," "that's a weight off my shoulders," "I've got butterflies in my stomach," "that sinking feeling," "chin up." Given this, it makes sense that changing your stance can shift your way of being. In her 2012 TED Talk, social psychologist Amy Cuddy introduced the idea of high and low power poses. Her research showed how posture can change a person's biochemistry—an open, relaxed, and expansive position increased testosterone by 20 percent and reduced stress hormones by a quarter, encouraging relaxation, confidence, and assertiveness. The effects of physical adjustments can be seen when a lack of energy almost dissuades a person from going to an exercise class from which they later emerge buzzing and revitalized. Similarly, deciding to sit down in the middle of the day might result in someone falling asleep. In a range of studies, psychologist Erik Peper found that when people stood straight and looked up they were likely to feel stronger, more energized, and more positive than when slouching. In collapsed positions, participants tended to experience increased access to negative memories and cognitive ability was impeded.

Physical and Nonphysical

Brain researchers Alyce and Elmer Green, who originated biofeedback—a technique used to gain control over involuntary bodily functions—and who also happen to be married, wrote in their 1970 paper: "Every change in the physiological state is accompanied by an appropriate change in the mental-emotional state, conscious or unconscious, and conversely, every change in the mental-emotional state, conscious or unconscious, is accompanied by an appropriate change in the physiological state." Like an efficient PA, the body vigilantly observes your mental babble, preoccupations, and body language to work out how best to serve you in any given moment. Mindfully observing these aspects of the self can give greater autonomy and improve mind–body communication.

USING THE BODY TO IMPROVE YOUR MOOD

1. Find Your Go-To Moods

While there's an array of ways of being that are available to adopt, there are also comfort zones—those moods slipped into without a thought.

Write down all the feelings you've had over the past couple of weeks.

....

....

....

....

....

....

....

Take a look at your list and identify the most common feelings—perhaps three or four. These are likely to be your go-to attitudes, the comfortable slippers of your emotional wardrobe. Note them here.

....

....

....

....

....

TRY THEM ON

Just as you would with an outfit, get into these mindsets and see how they look on you.

- Stand in front of the mirror.
- Choose a state.
- Remember when you felt this sensation.
- Allow your body to morph into the shape of this frame of mind.

Describe how your reflection looks in the mirror.

....

....

....

....

Notice how you feel in this position. Record your thoughts.

....

....

....

....

....

....

....

Have fun with this exercise. Look at the list again and, using the same process, examine the other variations of yourself. You could even try on attitudes you'd like to manifest. If you don't remember ever channeling those attitudes, think about others who do and mimic their body language as you pose.

CHOOSE A DIFFERENT OUTFIT

Changing posture can bring a fresh outlook, activate empowering hormones, improve problem-solving skills, and provide the confidence to use them.

Think of a time when you felt less capable than you might have liked. Note it down here.

....

....

....

....

As you reflect on it, let your body find the shape it held at the time. Hold onto it while you become aware of your experience.

Now recall a time when you were resourceful.

....

....

....

....

While you relive it, allow your body to find a fitting expression of those feelings. Stay this way and observe what it feels and looks like.

Go back to the first memory, but this time adopt the resourceful stance. What differences do you notice?

....

....

....

....

2. Transform Your State

Have you ever played the word game where one word becomes another by changing a single letter at a time? For example, getting from "rage" to "calm" might look like this:

- Rage
- Rale
- Bale
- Balm
- Calm

Similarly, the shift from one disposition to another requires a sequence of physical movements, steps where you can uncover your own path from state to state.

1. Choose a feeling from your list on page 28 you'd like to be able to move out of—for example, sad—and look at where you want to get. This could be glad. Identify two (or up to four) states in between. In this example, they might include quiet and content.

2. Write these four states on large pieces of paper and place them on the ground, like stepping stones. Make sure you leave enough room to progress from one to the next.

3. Begin at the first state or stepping stone, intuitively finding a way of carrying yourself that represents that word. Be guided by your body rather than your mind. Once you have it, take note (so you can find it again), then shake it off and move to the next stone, where you repeat the process.

4. Walking on each in turn, ease into the state with your body and find a posture that fits. Make sure you are clear about your body's shape for each one.

5. When you have moved to the final stone, go back to the beginning and repeat the exercise. In this way, you build pathways to guide you to resourceful emotional states.

6. Practice transitioning through the physical forms until your movements feel fluid and natural.

7. In your final incarnation, you could include a gesture you associate with this expression of yourself. You can use it as a shortcut whenever you need it.

A Mindful Compass

Integrity is something that's learned at a young age and built on throughout life. Sometimes finding the balance between what you think is right compared to what you follow because of external influences requires a deeper look within.

Integrity—a powerful word, bestowed upon those deemed to have demonstrated moral values and frequently linked to heroic gestures and acts of bravery. What often goes unnoticed are the small integrity-building actions of everyday life which, left unchecked, can disconnect body and mind and affect well-being. Derived from the Latin word *integer*, meaning whole or complete, integrity is a tool that does exactly what it says. When personal integrity is ignored, the line of communication between actions and gut is muffled. Conversely, practicing integrity on a daily basis will strengthen those lines, facilitating a direct dialogue within the self. This open dialogue is the key to connecting to deep desires and unleashing the strength required to move toward them.

The Role of Trust

A person with integrity is deemed trustworthy and also tends to possess strong self-trust—where they can fully rely on themselves to handle life. Without this, the ability to follow the body's important soft cues would be nonexistent. When these are ignored, they can transform into anxiety, sleeplessness, and physical pain. When integrity is intact, it's possible to build the necessary self-trust to pay heed to soft cues and act in ways perfectly aligned with a desired path.

OUTSIDE INFLUENCES

In the overstimulated Western world, it's almost impossible not to hear others' opinions. Awareness of these influences will help to differentiate what's right for you versus what you have learned.

Childhood Teachings

Most people learned right versus wrong in childhood, soaking up instructions from parents, teachers, mentors, or guardians. These adult figures provide the moral compass while the child's personal code is still being developed. Your ability to distinguish right from wrong remains intact. But can you recognize *your* right from *your* wrong? It might differ from those of your early role models, which means following what you were taught as a child is often not enough. Connecting to what is right for you now is the solution.

Societal Norms and Acceptability

Society has its own set of rules which, if followed, may divert a person from their desired path. It has the power to throw for a loop anyone without a solid grasp of their own personal integrity. For example, doing whatever it takes to get ahead, regardless of the cost to others, is often deemed perfectly acceptable. It may even be encouraged. Yet for many, doing so means they will have to ignore their soft cues (see step 2 on page 37).

Loved Ones

When doubtful about any action, you might ask others for their opinion. Although your gut may say one thing, you may want to seek justification to confirm or deny your instinct. Advice, whether solicited or otherwise, must be taken with a grain of salt. Suppose you are in a bind at work and know the only way to meet a deadline is to cut corners, creating extra work for a colleague. You know this will feel wrong, but you ask a friend for advice anyway. Filled with their own biases, they tell you they would go for it. You heed their advice and act accordingly, only to be diverted from your personal integrity. In this scenario, if you had listened to your gut, you may not have met your deadline. Your personal integrity, however, would not have been jeopardized. This doesn't mean someone else's advice is inevitably wrong, but in some circumstances, it can confuse a situation and has the potential to exacerbate internal turmoil.

HOW TO NURTURE INTEGRITY

There are many ways to discover and explore integrity. Here are a few. Choose the ones that work for you and spend as much time on each as suits your needs. They can be amended or followed exactly—this is your journey of discovery.

1. Practice Light Awareness

Be inquisitive. Throughout the day, take note of your interactions. This is a time of learning. There's no need to change your habits. Instead, view them without judgment. Jot down your findings as you go throughout the day or all at once in the evening. Do what you feel will inform your understanding best.

What opportunities for strengthening integrity did you have today?

....

....

....

....

....

....

....

....

....

....

....

....

....

....

2. Recognize Your Feelings

Connect with your body. Take time to notice your reponse to each interaction on the left. Does your stomach turn or your jaw clench? How long do these feelings remain? These discoveries will become soft cues for future encounters.

How did you feel about these opportunities to build integrity? Pay attention to any physiological changes, especially if they were not in line with your thoughts.

....

....

....

....

....

3. Challenge One at a Time

Keep it simple. When you have a grasp of how certain actions make you feel, choose one behavior that you'd like to change. The others will remain mentally present, but try to keep your choice at the forefront of your thoughts. One suggestion is to write positive reminders for yourself. For example, if your choice is to try to gossip less, write a note on your bathroom mirror or cell phone's lock screen that reads: "I will speak highly of others today." When you have a solid grasp on this particular action, move on to any others you want to address.

What would you like to change? How will you do this in a way that honors you and those around you?

....

....

....

....

....

....

4. Take Inventory

Congratulate yourself. Questioning your actions in this way takes courage and strength. Allow yourself the time you need to recognize—and celebrate—your accomplishments.

Jot down your accomplishments here—don't hold back! This is a time for acknowledging your wins.

....

....

....

....

....

....

....

....

....

....

....

....

....

....

....

....

NAVIGATING THE TRAPS

There are numerous scenarios that can strengthen or crush integrity. While everyone has varying principles based on different needs, there are some common situations where these principles are put to the test.

1. Gossip

Imagine for a second you're sitting in a cafe with a good friend, sipping hot beverages and chatting about life, love, work, and family. Suddenly, the conversation turns to a former acquaintance, and your friend relays a story that paints them in an unflattering light. Their comments make you feel awkward, but you nonetheless carry on with the conversation, swapping mean insults about the person. It's a common scenario in the workplace, at home, in the grocery store, on public transport, and on evenings out with friends. Bad-mouthing others may feel as though it gives a closer connection between the gossips. In reality, it's a false bond that hurts three people: the person you're speaking about, the person you're speaking to, and you. It dents personal integrity.

Think of a time you've been in this situation. How did you feel?

....

....

....

....

What did you do? Go along with the conversation or hold back? Why?

....

....

....

What would you do differently next time?

....

....

....

2. White Lies

Often regarded as an acceptable form of bending the truth, a white lie tends to go unnoticed. They're told to avoid conflict, spare feelings, get ahead, or to escape unpleasant feedback. Although mostly seen as trivial, they're the opposite and can create an environment of distrust. Importantly, they suggest you are not to be trusted. There are many scenarios where a white lie might be considered an option. You might have been working hard, for instance, and feel you need a day off. You believe your employer would disapprove, so your first thought is to say you have a cold and need to rest. You actually have several options. Asking yourself "What feels good to say?" followed by "What is my employer's business versus what is personal to me?" are good starting points. There's a difference between telling a white lie and not sharing information you feel belongs to you and only you. With this in mind, perhaps saying "I'm not feeling well" is a viable alternative to the white lie in this scenario because you are feeling overworked, unwell, and need personal time.

What white lies have you told recently that you could have worded differently?

....

....

....

....

....

How would you change your response next time?

....

....

....

....

....

3. Inauthentic Words

Reliability, trustworthiness, and authenticity are three fundamental aspects of solid integrity. Keeping your word plays a huge role in other people's trust as well as your own self-trust. If you've ever felt guilty after letting someone down, showing up late, or breaking a promise, you have felt a soft cue. It's there to let you know the action hasn't gone unnoticed. Saying "yes" when you mean "no" or even exaggerating excitement are also ways in which integrity is eroded. You may, for example, enthusiastically commit to an event despite having doubts that you'll be able to make it. This is easily avoided by saying you'd love to go but need to check the date first. There will always be times when it's necessary to postpone or cancel plans, but it will be done within a life of authenticity.

Have you said any inauthentic words recently? Why did you say them?

....

....

....

....

....

....

Did you feel a soft cue? If so, what was it?

....

....

....

....

....

....

What would you say or do next time?

....

....

....

....

....

....

....

....

....

....

....

....

....

....

....

These new discoveries can seem overwhelming at first. Once you note one action, though, many others will follow. During this time, it's important to stay grounded, and remember, you are human first and foremost. Everyone makes mistakes. Everyone slips. Perhaps try replacing "I should have . . . " with "I will do my best."

Freedom of the Senses

When worries seem mountainous, tuning into mindfulness and focusing on what you can feel, hear, and see can bring peace, calm, and balance.

When you're overwhelmed with worry your mind is somewhere else. Your body may be standing in line at the grocery store or sitting at your desk, and you may look like you're listening to another person speaking, but you're not really there. Your thoughts and attention are far away. You're thinking about a conversation you had, replaying a meeting at work, or pondering a task you could have done better. You're in the past, remembering an event, going over it, looking for clues, wondering how you could have acted differently, secondguessing what other people meant by their words, their glance, or their body language. Or you're in the future exploring possible scenarios for occasions and conversations that haven't happened yet, thinking through all the ways they could go wrong, how you could mess up, what calamity could befall you or your loved ones, how stressed and scared you could feel. And as you think about it, you feel it as if it's real right now. You don't know what's going to happen but you have ideas that seem plausible and you're ready with your response of "Yes, but what if?" for anyone who challenges you. Including when you challenge yourself.

Loss of Control

For those who don't worry too much, this probably seems stressful and exhausting, and feels like a waste of time. And they would be right. It's no fun fretting about what did happen and what might happen. It's not logical, it often doesn't make sense, it serves no beneficial purpose. Yet once the worrier's mind spirals off it feels like thought control is lost. That's what it seems like, but it isn't true. You do have a say in what your mind does and to what it gives its attention. Yes, in a matter of milliseconds the brain can fast-forward to a range of awful scenarios, which isn't easy to stop, but once you become aware of where your mind has run off to—when you notice you're spiraling into frightening thoughts—you can hop back into the driving seat and reclaim the steering wheel.

Stop the Spiral

You can make a conscious decision to bring your thoughts out of the past or future and into the here and now—into what is real and true in this world and in this moment. It's at this point that the spiraling brain will start to slow down, the stressful feelings will ease, and the fretting will peter out. So, how do you stop thoughts spiraling off into worry? First of all, this is not about stopping them. Tell yourself not to think of an elephant wearing a blue tutu and a tiara, and all you can think of is an elephant wearing a blue tutu and a tiara. This is about redirecting attention to focus on the present moment, not about trying to block out worrying thoughts. By refocusing attention, you give the brain a rest because you're not focused on the worry.

Mindfulness in Action

To refocus your attention, you practice mindfulness. This will help to ease stress, calm the mind, and soothe worries. Incorporating mindfulness into everyday life empowers you to spend more time noticing what's going on and finding enjoyment in what's happening in your life. It also helps to build resilience and manage stress. There are many ways to practice mindfulness in different situations for many reasons. On the next page is a technique you can practice any time you find yourself going over and over a past event or fretting about something that hasn't even happened. It's simple, you don't need props, no one needs to know what you're doing, and you can practice it anywhere, at any time, whether you're sitting alone at your kitchen table, on a crowded train, in a busy office, or walking along the street. It is a micro-mindfulness moment that can help you notice more and worry less.

TAKE A MOMENT

Bring your attention to your feet. Feel their pressure on the ground. Pay attention to each foot—how your weight is shared between them, how your feet feel, and whether they're in socks or shoes. There's no need to form an opinion on or change anything about them. You're simply noticing your feet, one at a time, giving them your attention rather than your worries.

1. Feel

If you were deep in worry when you began this exercise, you will find your mind pulling back to previous thoughts, returning to those worries. When you notice this happening, however many times, simply bring your attention back to your feet, their weight, their existence. Don't get irritable. Just notice you've drifted to worrying thoughts and bring your attention to the exercise.

Now bring your attention to each part of yourself in turn, through a mindful body scan. What sensations can you feel? Jot them down.

....

....

....

....

....

....

....

....

....

....

....

2. Hear

The next step is to move your attention from your feet to what you can hear. It could be conversation, traffic, stairs, or music on the radio. Single out and notice each one in turn. You don't need to identify who's making the sound or imagine what could be going on to create the noise. Just observe it. If you're in a quiet space, notice if your clothes make a sound as you breathe.

What can you hear? Write it down in a stream of consciousness.

....

....

....

....

....

....

....

....

....

....

....

....

....

....

....

....

....

3. See

Now you're going to move your focus again, this time bringing your attention to what is visible to the eyes. Name what you can see either out loud or in your mind—for example, a red door, a cracked sidewalk, a motorbike, white sneakers, a lamppost, a street sign—one by one. When your mind darts off to your worry again, bring it back to what you can see around you.

What can you see? Note them down here in a stream of consciousness.

....

....

....

....

....

....

....

....

....

....

....

....

You can move through feeling, hearing, and seeing, taking each one in turn, as many times as needed. Give your attention to something you can feel, then one sound you can hear, then name one item you can see, then back to what you can feel again. Your mind will pull away many times. This is normal. When you notice your thoughts have moved away from your senses, simply come back to what you can see, hear, or feel.

The Power of Anger

Used in the right way, this emotion has the ability to liberate and even to heal—but it requires a careful balance.

Anger is one of the most powerful emotions and, as such, can be one of the most destructive. It can cause rifts between family members or friends and be responsible for the ending of relationships. If you've ever witnessed explosive scenes of anger, either involving yourself or others, then you'll naturally be wary of this intense emotion. It needs careful handling, but is there a positive side to it?

What Is Anger?

Anger is energy. Many experts view anger as a normal, healthy reaction, claiming it can even be healing. Therapist Dr. Ronald Potter-Efron describes it like this: "You're walking down a path, and there's a boulder in your way, and if you get angry, then maybe you have enough strength to push the boulder out of the way. When people feel threatened, or come across an obstacle, anger is a natural response to help them move toward it."

Anger as Fuel

Arun Gandhi spent two years living with his grandfather Mahatma Gandhi, which inspired him to write a book, *The Gift of Anger*. His grandfather taught him how to see anger as a positive emotion. "Anger is to people like gas is to a car," Mahatma said. "It fuels you to move forward to get to a better place . . . Anger helps us to define what is just and what is unjust." But how can you ensure this anger is used as fuel, rather than to say or do things that are later regretted? Dr. Potter-Efron explains that when you get angry your body goes into a fight-or-flight response. The limbic system is activated and your heart rate, respiration, and blood flow to muscles increases. When there's no real danger, the frontal cortex and hippocampus shut down this response, which prevents a person acting out their anger. But sometimes it can be hard to override, particularly if a person feels extremely threatened.

The Root of Anger

Anger has its roots in fear. Often the feeling of being threatened goes back to childhood. Do you ever find your reactions, or those of loved ones, seem out of proportion to a given situation? Do small things, such as a colleague not replying to an email or a friend forgetting a coffee date, make you fly into a rage? Is your response dependent on how stressed you feel? Both present-day stress and past trauma can increase a sense of being threatened and prompt an angry outburst.

Role of Stress

Somatic experiencing is a therapeutic process aimed at relieving the symptoms of post-traumatic stress disorder and is based on the work of Dr. Peter Levine. He observed animals in the wild and noticed that after a fight-or-flight response— once they knew they were safe—they would shake off the cortisol and physical tension. In societies where expressions of feelings are discouraged, humans have largely lost touch with this natural healing response. Many people are also constantly bombarded with low-level stress, and although there is no real physical danger, this can prompt a constant state of fight-or-flight. As a result, personal feelings, and those of others, tend to emerge in angry explosions.

Internalized Anger

Feelings of anger can also be internalized. Dr. Gabor Maté, a physician and expert on trauma, addiction, stress, and childhood, says many cases of chronic fatigue, autoimmune conditions, and fibromyalgia are related to internalizing anger. This ties into the idea of anger being fuel, which may turn inward when it isn't used constructively. But how do you walk the line between destructive expressions of anger and its use for positive healing?

STRIKE A BALANCE

1. Take Time Out

Dr. Potter-Efron recommends taking time out to process the immediate feeling of anger before responding. Don't try to solve problems when you're angry. Take slow, deep breaths and try repeating to yourself: "I'm calm, I'm at peace." Breathing slowly sends a message to the brain to produce less cortisol, which is a way of telling the system it can stop preparing for a fight-or–flight response.

Use this space to process your feelings of anger. Write down what the trigger was, thinking about whether it has its roots in a previous trauma.

....

....

....

....

....

....

....

....

....

....

....

....

....

2. Look for the Fear Beneath the Anger

"Asking yourself, 'What might I be scared of?' can give you a different set of choices about how to respond," claims Dr. Woollard, a consultant and child and adolescent psychiatrist. "You might be angry that something has not gone your way. But you may also be scared that you might be blamed or hurt as a result. Recognizing this might allow you to think and act differently."

Now think about that trauma and how it relates to fear. Write down affirmations that validate your reaction.

....

....

....

....

....

....

How might you think and act differently next time?

....

....

....

....

....

....

....

3. Write It Out

Buddhist monk Thich Nhat Hanh suggests writing a letter to your angry self, "two or three pages, to show that you recognize his or her presence and will do everything you can to heal his or her wounds." Processing your anger on paper allows your unconscious to express whatever it needs to express without judgment or censorship. It can also help you to step back and evaluate your behavior and emotions, and to explore solutions. Ask yourself what needs to change in your life.

Write your letter to your angry self here. How can you create change?

....

....

....

....

....

....

....

....

....

....

....

....

....

....

....

....

....

....

....

....

....

....

....

....

....

....

....

....

....

....

If you find you are frequently getting angry, professional help may be necessary for you to get to the root of the issue. Visit your doctor or seek counseling services in your area.

Are You Too Selfish?

The balance between positive self-care and selfishness can be a difficult one to get right.

Selfishness is something that's easy to have a natural tendency toward. Life often feels like a dog-eat-dog situation, and it can seem less complicated to look out for number one: yourself. Indeed, there are times when you're actively encouraged to care for yourself above others. There is a fine line between self-care and selfishness, though, and you might know a person who treads heavily in that region of self-absorption. They may start every conversation with "I," always take the last cookie but never buy a new pack, often seem to be in a drama more sensational than anyone else, and rarely ask how you are. Maybe that someone is even you.

What Does it Mean to be Selfish?

Cara Hooper is an experienced personal and executive coach. She regularly helps people through challenges and change. "The people I have worked with over the years have defined 'selfish' as those who repeatedly put their own needs first, to the detriment of others," she says. "I believe, however, that the concept points more to a common human value of respect."

As a community-driven species, mutual respect tends to pay dividends for everyone, and there's much to be gained from healthy connections. Cara explains, "When we dish out respect, we quite rightly expect it back." Who doesn't want to feel respected in relationships and interactions? Sometimes you need to give people the benefit of the doubt, though—did they deliberately ignore you in the street, or had they forgotten their glasses? Cara continues, "A couple of selfish acts could well be mistakes or good old development opportunities, but a repeat offender may not know how to collaborate effectively in some relationships or, in plain speak, may act selfishly."

Effect on Relationships

Being around a selfish person can be draining, and over time it can become an unfulfilling friendship—one which you feel inclined to let go. In the case of close family, it can be infuriating and frustrating. For the selfish person in question, it can be hard to understand the cause of lost relationships and why friends eventually become unavailable. Cara says, "If someone is being too selfish they may wonder why either conflict or distance is impacting a relationship or, indeed, many relationships."

What Causes Selfishness?

Selfishness is motivated by many things. Sometimes a person's life experiences and circumstances can cause them to build walls or become inward-facing. Mental illness can also be a trigger. Sometimes it's simply personality differences—after all everyone is wired uniquely. Scientific research has shown that activation of the area of the brain known as the dorsolateral prefrontal cortex triggers self-control—and can affect whether someone keeps selfish impulses under control. While some may lean more easily into selfishness than others, it's not to say that it's impossible to turn back the tide and find a new way of thinking. You can challenge your own behaviors (if you want to) and make positive changes.

Canada-based business process improvement manager Kolyanne Russ says, "What my past experiences [have] taught me is that selfishness derives from thinking that our problems are worse than everyone else's and no one can understand us. However, if we take the time to reflect and observe other lives around us, we quickly realize that our problems are not bigger; they're just different. There will always be someone else who experiences worse situations than you and I." While it's important not to fall into overanalyzing yourself or self-sabotage, a little self-reflection can be useful. Although, as Cara says, "I have noticed that those who worry they might be acting selfishly really do not need to worry."

Is Selfishness Always a Bad Thing?

Shaelyn Pham is a psychologist, speaker, and author of the book *The Joy of Me: The Art of Being Selfish*. She disagrees with the negative label put on selfishness but recognizes that there is an important distinction to be made between self-care and being inconsiderate of others. "It's important to define the art of being selfish. A major lesson many of us carry from childhood to adulthood is that being selfish is 'bad.' Being selfish means we don't care about others, only ourselves—or so we're told. All our lives we've been taught not to be selfish, but being selfish doesn't mean you have to be inconsiderate of others or hurt them in the process. Self-compassion or self-love and selfishness cannot exist without one another. They are two faces of the same coin. The path to self-love can only be achieved through the art and act of selfishness."

Shaelyn says that when selfishness doesn't hurt or disrespect another person it can be a positive trait. "The art of being selfish is your ability to attend to the wants and needs of your body, heart, and soul to protect your happiness," she says. "No one else can make you happy. The only person who can make you happy is you. When you're focusing on yourself, you're taking responsibility for your own happiness. Hence, I want you to selfishly take care of your needs and to meet them so that you don't end up looking to others to fulfill your desires. You can't make your happiness someone else's responsibility."

Put Yourself First

This statement is often misunderstood—looking after number one is not a bad thing when there's giving as well as receiving. Negative selfishness is about one-sided transactions, and that's when being selfish becomes a bad thing. Instead, think of the advice you are given on an aircraft—adjust your own oxygen mask before assisting others.

ARE YOU BEING TOO SELFISH?

Being more self-aware is the first step to spotting the signs. Ask yourself the following questions and write down your honest answers.

What did you do today that could have been too self-centered?

....

....

....

Is there anything you could have done differently?

....

....

....

During a recent conversation, was it balanced or did you speak more than the other person?

....

....

....

Why was this? Was it a one-off—or does this one-sided style of conversation happen regularly?

....

....

....

WAYS TO GET THE BALANCE RIGHT

The following suggestions will help you to find that fine line between selfish and self-care.

Understanding
Understand that not everything revolves around you. Your priority is not necessarily the same as another person's—they have their own urgent tasks and challenges to deal with. Reminding yourself of this when you need something from someone else can help ease frustrations.

Awareness
Be aware of your surroundings and the words you use toward others. Remember the word *respect* and pause a little more to think before you speak.

Giving
Be a giver, not just a receiver. This doesn't need to be of physical things; it can be time spent listening. Becoming a good listener as well as a good talker will help to make you a better friend.

Empathy
Have empathy for others by taking a moment to think before judging or weighing in with advice. Put yourself in another's shoes and ask questions to better understand your friend or loved one's dilemma.

Acceptance
Don't live for validation from others. It can be easy to yearn for validation and acceptance, and this can be a slippery slope to self-absorption. Instead have faith in yourself and your own abilities—and give compliments to others where they are due. You'll find they come back on their own.

Truth or Lie?

There's a fine balance between telling a few white lies here and there and being a compulsive avoider of the truth—but how can you differentiate between the two?

No matter how hard you try, it's virtually impossible to tell the whole truth the whole time. People tell lies for all sorts of reasons, whether it's to protect someone's feelings, to make themselves appear more popular or successful, or to cover their tracks. Although these white lies are generally deemed acceptable if they're used on rare occasions and can be easily explained when confronted, if you're not careful, you can tip the balance and end up getting a reputation as someone who's a compulsive liar. Your lying can define you and cause others to stop respecting your opinion or believing a word you say in future. That lack of trust can ruin relationships beyond repair.

What If You're Being Lied To?

On the flip side, being on the receiving end of someone else's lies can be particularly distressing. When you suspect a friend, colleague, or partner is not being truthful, it can bring on a series of negative emotional responses. Firstly, you'll be desperate to get to the truth, then you'll wonder why they felt they couldn't be honest with you, and finally, you'll wonder what other lies they've been telling. You may be left asking whether you can trust them again. But before you jump to conclusions, it's worth remembering that not all lies are malicious.

White Lies

People lie through fear, to improve their image, or to save face. When a close friend or family member asks for your opinion on their latest hairdo or trendy new item of clothing, they don't necessarily want to hear your honest opinion—what they're actually asking you for is reassurance that they've made the right decision. If you truly think their dramatic new haircut makes them look like Mr. Bean, then it's probably not a good idea to say so unless you are sure they can take a joke, or you think the haircut could be rescued with a few clever styling tips. Instead, you may find yourself uttering classic platitudes such as, "Yeah, it really suits you." Of course, this can backfire if others disagree and your friend then comes back demanding to know why you weren't honest. As the old saying goes, you can't please all of the people all of the time. It's usually a case of weighing the pros and cons, and more often than not, it will depend on how well you know the person.

Tangled Webs

People also lie to avoid punishment, so admitting you've made a mistake is often hard because no one likes to appear incapable or untrustworthy, especially if it affects your status in a work environment. The instinct is often not to tell the truth and own up straightaway, but to try to rectify the situation before anyone else notices. The danger here is that as you try to cover your tracks, you're losing precious time and chances are someone will have spotted the mistake. The longer the delay, the harder it is to keep your integrity intact. The moment someone has proof that you lied to them once, the harder it is to convince them it was a one-off and it won't happen again.

So, as embarrassing or humiliating as it may be, owning up immediately and promising to try to solve the problem is the better option. Everyone makes mistakes, and most people understand this, but it's how you handle them that counts. The more honest you are, the less severely people will judge you.

Who's More Likely to Lie?

Being lied to by someone you trust and respect is particularly hurtful as it leaves you feeling betrayed and gullible for falling for their stories, and it can make you question your judgment. Certain personality types are more likely to tell lies. Extroverts are social creatures who enjoy being in the company of others and therefore have more opportunities to bluff or exaggerate. Sometimes they're also people-pleasers who are desperate to impress. But generally people with a lack of self-confidence or low self-esteem will be drawn to lie to compete with others who they view as superior or more popular. Some people enjoy the feeling of power it gives them to string you along with their fanciful and often dramatic stories. In fact, they weave such a complicated web of lies that they can actually begin to lose sight of the truth themselves.

Act of Betrayal

Anyone who's ever been betrayed in a loving relationship knows all too well the deep emotional pain felt after discovering someone you love and trust has been deceiving you. It's often the act of betrayal that hurts more than the details of what they've done. Once someone has betrayed you, it's difficult to put your trust in others and, sadly, that can have a snowball effect on future relationships. The natural instinct is to keep your distance from people who try to get close to you. But that means you're letting the betrayer influence your future life rather than remaining where they should be, which is in your past. Try not to judge everyone on the basis of one person who treated you badly, even if that means taking your time getting to know someone well before you place your trust in them.

WHAT'S THE ALTERNATIVE?

Lying can be habit forming, so you need to break the tendency as soon as possible. The good news is there are a few things you can do to help yourself.

1. Recognize the Triggers

First, try to identify the situations, emotions, places, or people that tend to cause you to avoid telling the truth. For example, you may find yourself lying when you're anxious about your abilities in the presence of certain people you find intimidating. Once you recognize the triggers for your lies, you can avoid them or find a way to confront them with honesty.

What are your triggers? Note them below.

....

....

....

....

....

....

....

....

....

....

....

....

....

2. Boost Your Self-Esteem

If you suspect your lying stems from a lack of self-confidence, it may help to build your self-esteem. Repeat the following affirmations to yourself for a self-esteem boost:

- *I respect myself, and others appreciate me.*
- *There's absolutely nothing out of my reach.*
- *I can have everything I want in life if I put my mind to it.*
- *I am doing a great job.*
- *I attract wonderful things into my life.*
- *I am whole and complete.*
- *Nothing can get in the way of my belief in me.*
- *My goals are already being accomplished.*
- *I am creative, strong, powerful, brave, and inspired.*
- *I love who I am and who I am becoming.*
- *I have much self-worth and inner beauty.*

3. . . . and Breathe

If you suffer from nerves and have a tendency to blurt out untruths in a blind panic, take a deep breath first and think carefully before you speak. Don't put yourself under pressure to give a definitive answer immediately, but visualize the conversation in your head and think about the potential questions you're likely to be asked before giving honest explanations. Choose your words carefully and keep your points as clear and concise as possible without being sidetracked. Ask yourself why you feel the need to lie and remember how destructive telling untruths can be in the long run.

Do you remember a time when you blurted out a lie in a panic? What was it?

....

....

....

....

....

How did you feel after?

....

....

....

....

What would you do or say differently next time?

....

....

....

....

Why did you feel the need to lie? Be as honest as you can.

....

....

....

....

....

....

....

....

....

TELLTALE SIGNS

Body Language
Liars often pull their body inward to make themselves feel smaller and less noticeable. They may become squirmy and try to hide their fidgety fingers from you.

Facial Expressions
Look out for any subtle changes in their skin coloration to a pinker shade, flaring of nostrils, biting of their lip, or rapid blinking. These changes signify an increase in brain activity as the lying begins.

Vocal Clues
When people are lying, they'll often slightly change the tone of their speech or they might start speaking more quickly or slowly. Their sentences become more complex as their brain works harder to keep up with their story.

"To exist is to change, to change is to mature, to mature is to go on creating oneself endlessly."

Henri Bergson

Embrace Your Blank Canvas

Ready to try something new? Starting afresh in life can be overwhelming, but there are tools to make the transition easier.

Deciding to take a particular direction in life doesn't mean having to stick by that choice forever. Much like anything worth investing in, life is open to growth and interpretation, and as experience builds, priorities change, and tastes develop. Sometimes, what was once thought to be an ideal way to be can become less desirable as time goes on.

This evolution is natural and, ultimately, makes room for progress and maturity. Life experiences teach you what is and isn't personally important, and as a result, you might outgrow relationships, jobs, or a way of being. Perhaps even all three. That is when you might consider making big changes or contemplate starting afresh.

Chartered health psychologist Kika Partakis has fifteen years of experience supporting clients who face such decisions, "I often work with people who wish to readdress life priorities. It is normal to wonder whether you're happy with your current life or if you would like to try new things. In fact, it's healthy to do so."

Research the Options

According to Kika, anyone facing such decisions might start by breaking down the process into conceivable and manageable chunks. The key is in understanding why you wish to make changes. Once this is established, an adjustment is necessary because implementing those alterations might be difficult, particularly if it involves making the decision to leave behind a pivotal part of life, such as a relationship or career. This means researching possible new eventualities thoroughly is the second step, and it will help to combat any thoughts that the transition might be overwhelming or impossible.

"Emotions can run high as these are important reflections," says Kika, "so it's helpful to have a journal to write things down in order not to lose your train of thought. Leave your notes and come back to them later in the day with a clearer, more objective mind. You could also talk them through with a friend, partner, or professional to unpack those important points you're trying to understand."

The value in reflecting in this way is to investigate whether a complete overhaul is necessary. Instead, says Kika, it might show that small modifications could improve your quality of life. "I always advise [clients] to keep an eye on mental and physical fatigue," she says. "Fatigue itself doesn't necessarily mean it's time for a big change; however, it does suggest it's a moment to look at adjustments. This could be by stopping and asking for support, making time for yourself with friends, and introducing more self-care such as meditation or downtime. For some, however, such reflection might confirm that it is appropriate to move on."

Inner Conflict

By this stage, it can be hard to ignore that change is imminent. Unease, stress, and anxiety are all indications that something might need to give. To instigate an overhaul of any aspect of life is a serious decision, however, and can be unsettling. It's what often discourages people from making such changes, but the cycle of discontentment and fear can lead to destructive mental and emotional health issues. In contrast, once the decision is made, it can feel like a weight has been lifted, which in turn feels empowering, liberating, and exciting.

Stress management coach and trainer Sarah Clark says these myriad conflicting feelings are part of the natural process between contemplation and action, and that putting up with short-term discomfort can present greater rewards. In fact, human beings are more prepared for large life changes than many realize. "You are capable of drawing on courage you might not realize you have," says Sarah. "Starting again is part of the human condition. If you're feeling dissatisfied, don't view it as a negative, rather as taking action for something new.

"Think back to what is important to you because over time people can lose track of this. The good news is that whatever situation you find yourself in, there are always going to be opportunities. You can draw on strengths by tapping into character traits, willpower, and by working out what new information you need and what support would be most helpful. Like tuning a guitar, it's going to feel uncomfortable and not instantly great, but in the longer run you will be able to create [a life] of which you feel prouder."

Setting smaller, more achievable goals and celebrating your progress can also foster a sense of moving forward. Try to remember change doesn't happen overnight. Practicing self-compassion and doing things you enjoy, be that running, meditating, or sketching, will also help to keep you focused on the existing positive elements in your world.

Be Clear on What You Want

It can also be helpful to remind yourself that a life without change, contrast, or adjustment can become stagnant and the desire to learn, experiment, grow, and celebrate can be thrilling. Make peace with the fact you might not always feel strong and accept there'll be moments when you question if you were right to proceed. This is natural, but it's during those times that it's worth reminding yourself that having the courage to start again is inspiring in itself. Importantly, be prepared and positive about seeking help if the going gets tough.

Marieke Egan, a self-leadership and strategic life coach, says maintaining clarity on what you want to achieve is important for those struggling to make the transition, "Be clear on exactly what you want the outcome to be. Envisage in detail what this would feel, sound, and look like. Feel the difference between staying where you are compared to being in the more ideal situation. Allow your strength to come from the inner knowledge that where you are isn't the right place for you."

Give Yourself a Break

Embracing new starts isn't a failure, says Marieke, but the inevitable result of a situation or event that didn't produce a desired outcome. "Be kind to yourself and remember, failure is only a human judgment," she says. "Realize life is about learning, growing, and becoming a better version of yourself, and that this is exactly what you are enabling by making such changes. It's an amazing opportunity to live a life in better alignment with who you are."

Fundamentally, when fatigue or doubt about the situation creeps in, trust in your instinct. After all, it helped you to make the decision to change things in the first place. Marieke describes this rewarding challenge in a beautiful and humbling way: "Ultimately, there is only one certainty in life, and that is that life always changes. It is what makes things exciting. Make change your friend early on, and dance with it. This simple outlook will greatly help anyone to start afresh."

DO YOUR HOMEWORK

There are some questions to ask yourself when considering a big life change.

Why do I want to make this change?

....

....

....

....

....

....

If I don't do it now, will I regret it?

....

....

....

....

....

How do I feel when I think about making the change?

....

....

....

....

....

Am I doing this for me or for someone else?

....

....

....

....

....

What are the likely consequences?

....

....

....

....

....

TAKING THE LEAP

Here's how to turn the negative into a positive stepping stone.

- Experiencing restlessness, dissatisfaction, demotivation, anxiety, and fear on an ongoing and inescapable basis is an indication you might be out of balance with your core values and beliefs.

- When you take the steps toward change and you start to feel inspired, excited, enthusiastic, and motivated, it's a sign you are moving back into alignment and a better chance of contentment.

- Treat your inner feelings as your guidance system, and they'll tell you when you're on the right track.

Cooling Breath

Next time you find yourself getting hot and bothered, try this yoga breathing technique, called Sitali Pranayama, *or "Cooling Breath," to bring balance back into your day.*

- Sit in a comfortable seated position, spine upright and straight, shoulders relaxed and open. Gently rest hands on your knees, palms open and facing upward or fingers held in a mudra position. A popular mudra is chin mudra, where the first finger and thumb touch, forming the shape of a circle. The chin mudra is said to activate the area in the brain related to wisdom and knowledge.

- Sit for a moment, gently breathing in your regular breath, to allow your body to settle and your senses to relax and center.

- Breathing in, form a circular "O" with your lips. Curl your tongue, bringing up the sides to form a "U" shape. Gently push your tongue through the open circle your mouth has made so that it comfortably extends past the lips.

- Take a deep breath in through your mouth along your straw-like tongue, then slowly draw your tongue back into your mouth, close your lips, hold your breath, and breathe out through your nose. Repeat this technique to a simple rhythm, breathing in for a count of five, holding for a count of two, and exhaling for a count of five.

- If you are unable to curl your tongue, try an alternative yoga technique called *Sitkari Pranayama*. Simply bring your teeth together and inhale through the gaps in your closed teeth. Close your lips, hold your breath, and breathe out through your nostrils as above.

Please Your Knees

Used in most regular activities, this vital joint undergoes a lot of strain every single day of the year. Luckily, there are some easy-to-follow exercises to help boost balance and strengthen the knee, as well as the surrounding structures.

The knee is an important piece of the anatomical jigsaw, yet it's the part of the body that causes many problems for countless people, with the likelihood and the severity of an issue increasing with age. From general morning stiffness, to more serious conditions such as arthritis, knee issues can arise at any age and in any walk of life, often having a significant impact on everyday activities.

Complicated Structure

Think about your normal daily activities. It's likely that most will involve the knees in some capacity—going for a stroll, sitting at a desk, walking up the stairs—and that's before even thinking about bringing more strenuous pursuits into the mix. Hobbies such as running, gardening, or biking with friends place further demand on these joints, with every movement adding impact or stress to its complicated structure, which for some proves too painful even to contemplate. Maintaining healthy knees is important, given their vital role in even the most basic of human functions.

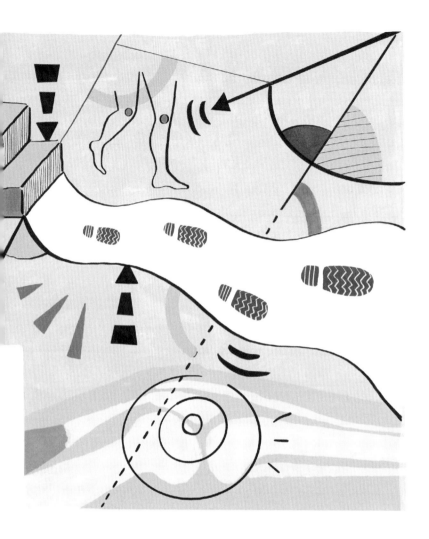

Inside the Joint

The knee is a large, complex joint, connecting the femur bone of the upper leg and the tibia bone of the lower leg. Through a range of motions such as bending, extending, and—to a lesser degree—rotating, the knee enables a range of movement and functions, supporting the weight of the human body in the process. Physiotherapist and yoga teacher Sarah Harrower explains, "The knee is a load-bearing joint and carries one to two times your body weight when walking or climbing stairs and up to an amazing three to four times during running." But it's not just the bones themselves that take the pressure. "Other important structures in the knee include ligaments, cartilage, fluids, and the fat pad," she adds. As there are so many delicate components, damage can occur easily, with a movement as seemingly innocuous as bending down to pick up something from the floor being a potential trigger for a sprain or strain.

Taking Care of the Knees

The great news is a lot can be done to help keep knees healthy and to protect against injury and pain. Much of this is preventative and maintaining good posture is key. Simple and straightforward exercises to increase resilience can reduce the likelihood of damage and the need for corrective action. Surprisingly much of this good work is achieved not by targeting the knee itself, but by strengthening and mobilizing other parts of the body, improving posture, and moving in a conscious way. Working with vital supporting muscles and tissues and keeping them in good working order can be key to avoiding pain, strain, and stiffness.

Supportive Structures

The strong muscles around the hips, for example, play an important role in ensuring good alignment of the knee, with weak or overly tight muscles having the potential to cause the knee to track inward or splay outward, often leading to incremental damage to the delicate tissues and bones contained within the knee. Likewise, tightness or poor mobility around the ankles and its supporting muscles—including those within the lower leg—causes restricted movement, leading to overcompensation of the foot, which often culminates in knee issues. Sarah says, "Stay active and vary the types of activity. If new to exercise, a graded approach is best so as not to overload. Listening to the body is key—gradually start to improve flexibility, strength, and balance before doing anything too challenging." There are many activities that can help, though just moving more is a great start. As Sarah says, "To keep a joint healthy, it must be moved."

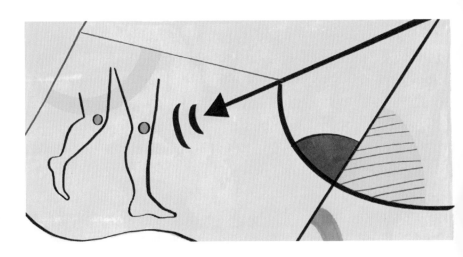

How Yoga Can Help

When practiced in a conscious, mindful way that works within the safe limits of the body, yoga is a great way of helping to keep the knees healthy via a combination of mobilization, strengthening, and elongation. Slower, steadier forms, such as traditional hatha and yin, are particularly beneficial as they invite this mindful approach to movement and alignment.

YOGA FOR THE KNEE

Here's a short sequence to try at home. Move slowly and gently through the postures, maintaining a rhythm of long, slow, and deep breathing throughout. It may initially be helpful to practice this sequence in front of a mirror to gain familiarity and awareness of the body's position.

1. *Tadasana*/Mountain Pose

Begin the sequence by standing strong in *tadasana*, also known as mountain pose. Hold for at least one minute to become centered and gain awareness of your body's position. This helps you properly align your knees in relation to the rest of your body.

- Stand with feet hip-width apart and parallel, toes pointing forward, knees facing forward and in line with the ankles.
- Visualize grounding down through your feet, but avoid collapsing.
- Keeping your knees soft, visualize a gentle opening across the backs of your knees, creating a sense of lengthening up and down your leg.
- Allow your arms to fall naturally and lightly by the sides of your body. Your biceps and thumbs face forward while your palms face your thighs.
- Visualize a thread passing through your body, up through the crown of your head, creating a sense of lengthening through your neck.
- Let the thread create lightness in your upper body—a gentle elongation from your waist up.
- While remaining alert and aware of the position of your body, relax into a rhythm of calm breath.
- Remain here for at least one minute.

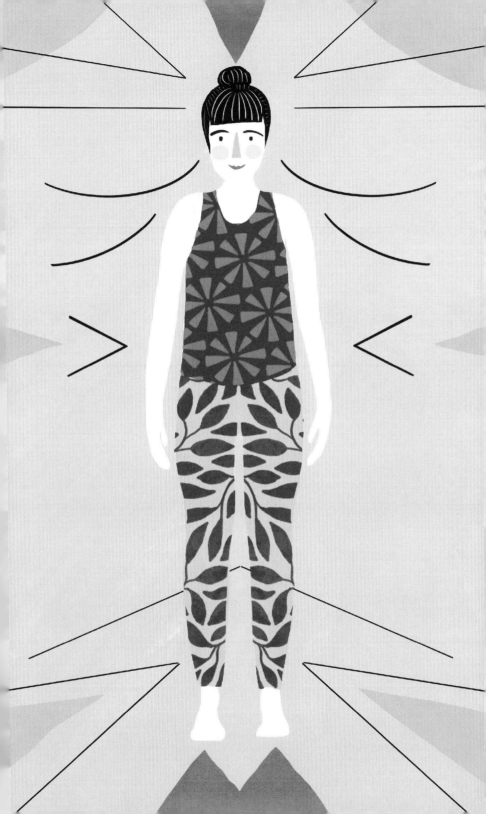

2. *Utkatasana*/Chair Pose

Utkatasana is a leg- and glute-strengthening pose, which might feel a little challenging at first but will become easier with continued practice (see illustration).

- From *tadasana*, raise your arms parallel above your head, with your palms facing each other.
- Lengthen through the fingertips and keep your shoulders relaxed and away from your ears.
- With an exhalation, slowly start to lower your body back and down—squatting as though you are about to sit on a chair with your body's weight in the heels. Move slowly and steadily, ensuring your knees remain parallel and behind your toes.
- Remain here for a count of five, maintaining a rhythm of calm breathing before slowly rising back to *tadasana* with an exhalation.
- Gently repeat this sequence, slowly and steadily moving between *utkatasana* and *tadasana* three times.

Knees tracking inward or outward are a sign to back up a little. Only lower down as far as good alignment is maintained—even the slightest of squats can make a world of difference.

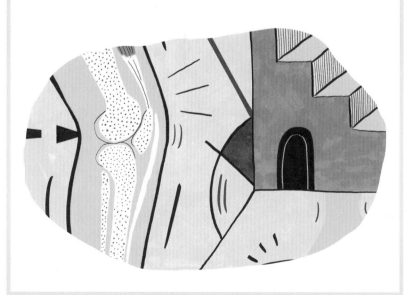

3. *Saaras Pakshi*/Stork Pose

This standing balance pose is also a good lower-body strengthener—an all-rounder that works your ankles, calves, thighs, and glutes. Balancing is also great for improving coordination.

- From *tadasana*, ensure stability through your left leg by grounding down through your foot, maintaining a slight bend in your knee to avoid overextending the joint.
- With your hips level and facing forward, slowly begin to lift your right foot with an exhalation.
- While maintaining good balance, continue to lift your right knee until your thigh is parallel with the ground.
- For a real test of balance, try experimenting with different arm positions. Options include arms relaxed by the sides, resting the hands on the hips, or raising your arms above your head with palms facing each other.
- Remain here for a count of five, maintaining a rhythm of calm breathing before slowly lowering your right foot back down to the ground to return to *tadasana* with an exhalation.
- Remain in *tadasana* for a count of five, becoming aware of the sensations of having both feet on the ground, before repeating on the other side.
- Gently repeat this sequence, slowly and steadily moving between balancing and *tadasana* on each foot three times.

Move slowly and stay relaxed, keeping your standing leg and foot strong but not clenched. Balancing can feel easier by focusing your gaze on a fixed point straight ahead. As your balance improves, try keeping your leg raised for longer periods, and once you master that, try this with your eyes closed for a real test.

4. *Baddha Konasana*/Butterfly

This seated posture lengthens the muscles along the insides of your thighs and groin area and relaxes the outsides of your glutes, relieving tightness that can contribute to knee problems (see illustration).

- Carefully lower down to a seated position. Place a cushion or blanket underneath your bottom to elevate your hips for greater comfort, if needed.
- Softly hold your ankles (or shins, if easier), then bring the soles of your feet together and draw your heels in toward your groin.
- Visualize grounding down through your hips, but try to avoid collapsing.
- Now, visualize a thread passing through your body and up through the crown of your head to create length and lightness in your upper body.
- Gently allow your hips to open by slowly and steadily lowering your knees outward and down toward the ground.
- Remain here for a count of ten, then softly begin to "butterfly" your knees up and down to loosen around your hips for another count of ten.

Avoid pushing down on your knees. They don't need to reach the floor, just to the point where a gentle elongation is felt along the insides of your thighs. Cushions or blankets can be placed beneath the outside of your thighs, if more support is needed.

5. Windscreen Wipers

This movement relieves tightness in your legs, hips, and groin, as well as providing a gentle twist along the sides of your upper body. It's a great way to ease down after strengthening postures (see illustration).

- From *baddha konasana*, use your hands to support the outside of each knee, slowly directing your knees in toward each other—as though closing a book—to hip-distance apart.
- Place the soles of your feet flat on the ground, also hip-distance apart.
- Place the palms of your hands down just behind your bottom, on either side of your hips, to support the weight of your body, though avoid collapsing in to your arms.
- With an exhalation, slowly rotate both your knees left toward the ground until a gentle elongation is felt along the outside of your right thigh, hip, and waist.
- Return to the center with an inhalation, before continuing over to the right with an exhalation.
- Gently repeat this sequence, slowly and steadily moving your knees from left to center and then to the right three times.

Always take some time to sit or lie still afterward to allow your body and mind to relax and absorb the benefits of the practice. As with all forms of movement, take great care to move within the limits of your body and stop immediately if you experience any pain. Always seek advice from a doctor or experienced physical therapist if you're unsure whether yoga is suitable for you.

Top of the List

Whether it's five minutes looking at the sky or half an hour lying on your bed listening to a podcast, try to add at least one soul-nurturing activity to your daily schedule.

The humble to-do list has the potential to organize a day of daunting responsibilities into something simple and tangible. It can alleviate anxiety about how much there is to be done (and how much time there is to do it) and provide a sense of balance, as well as one of reward, peace, and purpose—particularly in turbulent times or where the boundary between home and work is blurred. For many, thoughts of a to-do list bring to mind emails to be answered, work projects to be filed, and errands to be run. It's all the essential tasks to be fully completed before stealing some me-time, whenever that's possible. Instead of exclusively listing chores, however, what about adding activities that benefit personal well-being, affording them the same priority both on the page and in your mind? All the check marks are the same size, after all, irrespective of the scale or content of the tasks they represent.

Putting Yourself First

New York–based professional organizer Rashelle Isip, also known as the Order Expert, says incorporating well-being into a day's plan helps to prioritize the self. "It puts a focus on your goals rather than dealing with them later," she says. "It's forcing you to deal with them right now because otherwise, in the day-to-day minutiae of things, they can get lost."

Even for those who tend not to have daily schedules, making a list of things you're going to do for yourself can help to prioritize personal well-being, especially as the tasks can be anything that brings you pleasure, be that taking out your knitting, making yourself dinner from an underused recipe book, or listening to a podcast downloaded ages ago. You could think of it as a daily bucket list, the incentive being those satisfying ticks at the end of the day. The important thing is to make sure the activities genuinely make you feel better; otherwise, there's a danger they'll feel as laborious as a traditional to-do list.

TO-DO LIST

Reshape the Everyday

It's equally handy to remember that self-care and well-being aren't only present in tasks defined as enjoyable. They can also be found in the everyday routines already on your list, which makes them easier to achieve. In this case, it's more a case of reframing them so that "put away all the clothes draped over my chair" or "water the plants in my room" are turned into moments of contemplation. After all, whoever said a bubble bath was the only way to find inner quiet? And these everyday but less obviously enjoyable tasks can help to bring future calm without encroaching on a busy schedule. Nurturing a houseplant, for example, is said to boost mood and reduce stress, while cleaning is reported to relieve anxiety.

Don't Overfill

It's helpful not to cram too much onto your list, because while it can offer a sense of peace, it also has the potential to do the opposite. A 2019 survey of 1,353 people by transatlantic leadership training company VitalSmarts found that 60 percent of respondents had more than sixty tasks on their weekly lists, and more than half said they overcommitted because they didn't want to let themselves or others down. Being realistic about what can be achieved is essential for a list to work, even if it includes items that prioritize health and well-being.

Rashelle sees a schedule or list as merely a vessel: "It doesn't necessarily have to be filled for it to be important." She suggests thinking of it as you might a refrigerator. Whether it's full to the max or has only the essentials, it still performs its task of keeping the food fresh. Similarly, making sure a schedule isn't completely packed and removing unnecessary things can help stop a day from becoming too long and overwhelming. Ultimately, try to be realistic about what you have the emotional, physical, and mental capacity to do on any particular day.

REFRAMING YOUR TO-DO LIST

- **Brainstorm.** Get the ideas in your head down on paper so you can see them clearly.

- **Identify.** Work out what you want to do and break them down into more manageable, smaller tasks.

- **Incorporate.** Tack a new habit onto an existing one. If you wake up in the morning and have a hot drink, add "go for a walk" or "read thirty pages of my book."

MY SELF-CARE TO-DO LIST

Write down all the activities—including everyday ones that can be reframed as calming moments—that might be used to find inner quiet and nourish your soul. Then try to include at least one, whether that's "fold away the towels" or "listen to the birdsong," on your to-do list.

....

....

....

....

....

....

....

....

....

....

....

CREATE A ZEN ZONE

Turn a quiet space at home into your own private sanctuary,
somewhere you might meditate, journal, or just think about things
that you enjoy.

- Light scented candles.

- Play soothing music.

- Add soft cushions and your favorite blanket to snuggle into.

A Diet for Keeps

Tired of following draconian diets where everything is written in stone and life revolves around counting calories, fasting for days, or banishing carbs or protein? Throw the rulebook in the trash, break free, and create a balanced way of eating that works for you today—and for life.

There's always a diet craze promising to shed extra pounds, energize, and curb so-called bad food cravings for good. Most people have tried at least one diet, but despite starting out with good intentions, there's a fall from the wagon and a return to old habits. So, let's pause for a moment and consider whether a one-size-fits-all diet—where food types become demonized and are fed by an obsession to obey impossible rules—is truly the best option.

No One-Size-Fits-All Approach

When you think about it, no single diet is ever going to be right, or even healthy, for everyone. Few, for instance, can follow in British tennis player Andy Murray's footsteps and make their way through 6,000 calories a day, demolishing fifty pieces of sushi in one sitting. After all, the average Joe tends to be found sitting behind a desk, not smashing it on a tennis court! What's the alternative? Stop following everyone else's strategies for dietary success and embrace bio-individuality by designing your own way of eating. A personalized plan that works for you and complements your lifestyle. You know your body better than anyone else, so who better to make the rules?

Fling Away Fad Foods

It's time to ditch the predesigned diet formula that's tasteless, self-absorbed, and controlling (let's be honest, most people are probably going to end up cheating on it anyway) and instead find one that tickles the taste buds, caters to every need, and is a true keeper. Strip down any dietary theory and you'll find it comprises three principles—these will form the framework of your new way of eating. Just a little note before getting started: if you have any medical conditions or anxieties, do always check with your doctor first before making any radical changes to your diet.

THREE PRINCIPLES

In a nutshell, all dietary theories shift the source, balance, and timing of macronutrients, otherwise known as carbohydrates, proteins, and fats. So, what do these terms mean?

- Source describes where carbohydrates, proteins, and fats come from. While vegans are restricted to plant-based proteins only, Paleo dieters eat a lot of animal protein.

- Balance refers to the percentage of carbohydrates, proteins, and fats. For an average healthy adult, the suggested percentages are 50, 30, and 20 respectively.

- Timing is when to eat the carbohydrates, proteins, and fats. For some diets, you have several smaller portions a day, instead of three larger ones. Some diets may focus on one or two of these principles and be nonspecific about the third; others replace meals with smoothies and some stipulate cooking techniques such as baking or steaming, or leaving food raw.

MACRONUTRIENTS

What exactly are macronutrients? "Macro" comes from the Greek *makros* meaning large—and carbohydrates, proteins, and fats are all nutrients we need in large amounts to provide energy, which is measured in calories. While carbohydrates and proteins provide four calories per gram, fat is a high-density energy source and provides nine calories per gram. The recommended calorie intake will depend on your sex, age, height, weight, and lifestyle, but it's around 2,000 calories for women and 2,500 calories for men.

Carbohydrates

There are two types of carbohydrates: simple and complex. Simple carbohydrates, such as sucrose (table sugar), fructose (fruit sugar), and lactose (milk sugar), are generally digested and absorbed quickly, providing a burst of energy that is often followed by a slump. Complex carbohydrates, such as those found in whole grains, beans, and legumes, are digested and absorbed much more slowly, providing a steady stream of energy, keeping our batteries running throughout the day. There is one exception—fiber. This is found in foods like oats, bananas, and sweet potatoes. Although it's a complex carbohydrate, the body can't digest it, so it doesn't provide energy. But it still has multiple health benefits—it helps to control blood sugar, assists in weight-loss because it gives a feeling of fullness, slows carbohydrate metabolism, and helps with bowel movements.

Proteins

Proteins are large complex molecules that the body uses to make hormones, blood, enzymes, muscles, skin, hair, and nails, among many other elements. They form part of every cell in the body. Proteins aren't used as they are found in food, but are broken down into amino acids. There are twenty amino acids, eight of which are essential and have to be derived from food. Whereas animal proteins like meat, eggs, and dairy products are complete proteins because they contain all eight essential amino acids, many plant-based proteins like beans, legumes, and whole grains are incomplete proteins as they lack one or two. However, those missing in legumes are normally supplied in whole grains. If you do not consume animal protein, make sure you include different types of plant-based protein in your diet so the body gets all the essential amino acids it requires. Soybeans are one of the few sources of plant-based proteins that are complete proteins.

Fats

There are four types of fats: trans, saturated, monounsaturated, and polyunsaturated. Trans fats are produced artificially and are found in processed, fried, and baked foods. Try to avoid them as they can raise your cholesterol levels, increasing your risk of heart disease. Although they're not noted on food labels, you can usually spot them listed on ingredient lists as hydrogenated and partially hydrogenated vegetable oils. As a general rule of thumb, saturated fats found in food such as cakes, cookies, and pastries should be kept to a minimum as they can raise cholesterol levels. The exception to the rule is coconut as this has the opposite effect (even there, practice moderation). You can track your intake by checking food labels. The recommended maximum daily allowance of saturated fats is ¾ ounce (20 g) for women and 1 ounce (30 g) for men. Unsaturated fats are the healthy ones as they reduce cholesterol levels, lowering the risk of heart disease. Monounsaturated fats are found in olive oil, avocado, nuts, and seeds. Polyunsaturated fats include omega-3 found in oily fish and oils such as linseed oil and omega-6 is found in nuts and seeds as well as oils like sunflower oil. Both omega-3 and omega-6 are essential fatty acids, so if you don't get them through your diet, they need to come from supplements.

FIND WHAT WORKS FOR YOU

Now it's time to discover what source, balance, and timing works best for your body. A food journal is a useful way to keep track of your progress, allowing you to record which foods you're eating, what time you're eating them, and how you feel after you've eaten them. The type of food you consume has a huge impact on energy levels, concentration levels, and general sense of well-being. It's these feelings you need to tap into and become more aware of.

1. Food Diary
Start by tracking and listing your food intake for a week—this will give you a baseline from which to work. Note how you feel right after eating and then again two hours later.

MONDAY

Breakfast   Time

Food eaten ....

....

....

Feelings after eating ....

....

....

Lunch   Time

Food eaten ....

....

....

Feelings after eating ....

....

....

Dinner   Time

Food eaten ....

....

....

Feelings after eating ....

....

....

Snacks   Time

Food eaten ....

....

....

Feelings after eating ....

....

....

TUESDAY

Breakfast

Time

Food eaten ....
....
....

Feelings after eating ....
....
....

Lunch

Time

Food eaten ....
....
....

Feelings after eating ....
....
....

Dinner

Time

Food eaten ....
....
....

Feelings after eating ....
....
....

Snacks

Time

Food eaten ....
....
....

Feelings after eating ....
....
....

WEDNESDAY

Breakfast
Time

Food eaten ....
....
....

Feelings after eating ....
....
....

Lunch
Time

Food eaten ....
....
....

Feelings after eating ....
....
....

Dinner
Time

Food eaten ....
....
....

Feelings after eating ....
....
....

Snacks
Time

Food eaten ....
....
....

Feelings after eating ....
....
....

THURSDAY

Breakfast

Time

Food eaten

....

....

....

Feelings after eating

....

....

....

Lunch

Time

Food eaten

....

....

....

Feelings after eating

....

....

....

Dinner

Time

Food eaten

....

....

....

Feelings after eating

....

....

....

Snacks

Time

Food eaten

....

....

....

Feelings after eating

....

....

....

FRIDAY

Breakfast   Time

Food eaten ....
....
....

Feelings after eating ....
....
....

Lunch   Time

Food eaten ....
....
....

Feelings after eating ....
....
....

Dinner   Time

Food eaten ....
....
....

Feelings after eating ....
....
....

Snacks   Time

Food eaten ....
....
....

Feelings after eating ....
....
....

SATURDAY

Breakfast

Time

Food eaten

Feelings after eating

Lunch

Time

Food eaten

Feelings after eating

Dinner

Time

Food eaten

Feelings after eating

Snacks

Time

Food eaten

Feelings after eating

SUNDAY

Breakfast
Time

Food eaten ....
....
....

Feelings after eating ....
....
....

Lunch
Time

Food eaten ....
....
....

Feelings after eating ....
....
....

Dinner
Time

Food eaten ....
....
....

Feelings after eating ....
....
....

Snacks
Time

Food eaten ....
....
....

Feelings after eating ....
....
....

3. My Favorite Macros

From your food diary, you can create a list of proteins, carbohydrates, and fats that give you sustained energy, satisfy your taste buds, and make you feel great. Pay particular attention to sources that you don't usually incorporate in your diet.

Proteins:

....

....

....

....

....

....

Carbohydrates:

....

....

....

....

....

....

Fats:

....

....

....

....

....

4. Make a Bespoke Diet Plan

Once you have your list of favorite macronutrients, gradually start to shift the balance of your preferred foods. Ask yourself how many meals you'd like to eat and at what time of day. Make sure your choices complement your lifestyle. If you get up at 5:00 a.m., for instance, you might want to have two smaller meals in the morning to make sure you don't start to flag before lunchtime. Consider how active you are during the day and shape your diet plan around the nourishment your body needs to be at the top of its game.

My Diet Plan:

....

....

....

....

....

....

....

....

....

....

....

....

....

....

....

BE IN TUNE WITH YOUR BODY

If you tap into your body's innate wisdom, it should guide you to healthy food choices, but if you're constantly craving food you know isn't nutritious and makes you feel sluggish, then ask yourself the following questions.

What is my relationship to food and my body?

....
....
....
....
....
....
....

Do I let emotions impact my food choices?

....
....
....
....
....
....
....
....
....

How do I eat?

....

....

....

....

....

....

....

....

....

....

....

....

....

Study your answers. Sometimes it can be useful to seek outside advice to help you to explore them and find ways to shift triggers and behaviors. When the head is stuck in dietary dogma and focused on sticking to the rules, it can be hard to let go, tune into the body, and listen to its feedback. By allowing yourself space to create your own way of eating, you can begin to eat intuitively, bring awareness back into your body, and place trust in it that it will lead you to the right types of food. As you change so, too, will your diet, but all you have to do is revisit your framework and adjust the source, balance, and timing to meet your body's needs at the time.

Slow It Down

There's more to yoga than the physical aspects of turning yourself into a pretzel or sweating profusely through an energetic sequence. Incorporating slower forms in your practice can bring back the balance that's often lost when favoring more dynamic styles.

Sweat pours and your heart thumps while your muscles scream, "Please, no more!" and your head pleads, "Don't make me do this again." Yoga can get physical, with many classes geared toward faster and more dynamic forms, such as vinyasa and ashtanga, where participants use their practice as a cardiovascular workout. It's a wonderful way to boost your metabolism and get the endorphins pumping. Sometimes, though, it compromises form and the internal and external sensing that comes with the slower and steadier forms of practice, such as classical hatha or iyengar. Here, we explore the focus on union of body and mind presented by slow yoga.

Tune In to Yourself

The word *yoga* comes from the Sanskrit term for union or connection. Slowing things down presents the opportunity to connect with what's really going on inside—in this sense, a true union of body and mind. There is no competition, pushing, or forcing; it's just a beautiful way to tune in with physical sensations, the mind, emotions, and, ultimately, with yourself. Natasha Marchant is the founder of Gaia Lifestyle in Cardiff, Wales, a community space providing yoga, complementary therapies, and creative events as well as special retreats. She explains how she discovered the joys of the slower form. "It was the gentle nurturing practices that brought me home to myself. The slow movement of the body coordinated with the breath, the held postures, supported with bolsters and blankets. It was the essence of these practices that enabled me to find the space within my body, within my thoughts, within my breath."

Be Still

Slowing things down creates a physical quality of stillness. Stillness of the body cultivates a sense of presence—physically and mentally—which helps to sharpen the brain because it becomes easier to focus and quiet the chatter in the mind. By tuning in to the breath, it becomes softer and quieter as it settles into a rhythm and depth: deep, smooth, and steady—a beautiful experience. Calm breathing leads to a calm mind, which can be hard to find in today's hectic world. Restorative yoga, where the body is supported by props, including bolster cushions and foam blocks, allows you to relax into postures and is a haven for many. Natasha loves teaching it. "Supported backbends, forward bends, legs up the wall, and gentle twists are all just heaven when using a bolster, giving you the time to settle into your body and breath."

Emotional Release

While in stillness, difficult and uncomfortable feelings can arise as emotions that are sometimes swept under the carpet become prominent and noticeable. This is natural and, by allowing these feelings to come up, you can learn to accept them. Doing so lets you go with rather than against the tide. Approaching the experience with curiosity presents the opportunity for acceptance—that it's okay to experience these emotions irrespective of whether they're perceived as positive or negative. The process of accepting emotions allows them to pass.

Experience the Calm of Yin

With so many emotional and mental benefits, slower yoga presents a gentle and enjoyable way to relieve stress, boost your mood, and generally feel good. Jenny Shutt, a management consulting director from London, initially turned to yoga as a way to fill her free time while working overseas. These first experiences were with the more dynamic forms, but on returning home, she became curious about the other styles. Jenny explains, "I decided to go to a half-day yin yoga workshop. The philosophy was different: a cool studio, mainly sitting on the floor, holding poses for a minimum of five minutes. However, the euphoria I felt afterward was as good, if not better [than previous experiences]. I felt incredible when I'd finished the class."

Jenny experienced that magical sense of stillness for herself with the yin of a cooler and calmer approach, in contrast with the yang of hotter and more energetic styles. "I needed some balance in my life," she says. "I had changed jobs and was based in London full-time and getting increasingly anxious because of the environment and fast-paced nature of city life." The union helped to bring calm when it was needed.

Gentle Practice

The beauty of this approach is that it's accessible to anyone, regardless of previous yoga experience and level of fitness. It can involve sitting quietly in a chair, focusing on the breath while gently flexing the spine back and forth or taking easy sidebends and feeling the space this creates in the ribs. There are physical benefits to a steadier, slower method that is kinder to the body. Listening to what the body might need (and is capable of) and giving it the gentle attention it deserves allows the practitioner to tap into what's happening on a physical level. This awareness makes it easier to notice, pinpoint, and alleviate any "issues in the tissues" that might be masked by the huff and puff of more energetic endeavors.

Slow, Steady, and Stable

With steadier practice comes stability, which can help build physical strength, improve joint mobility, and develop strong yet supple muscles. Yoga teacher Natasha describes the transformative effects she witnessed while working with a student suffering the symptoms of fibromyalgia, which include chronic pain, tiredness, and mood disturbances. Natasha introduced her to a simple, slow, and steady practice. "She had tried various classes, but found that flowing sequences of weight-bearing asana left her exhausted and would trigger an inflammatory response in her body. Together, we experienced the subtlety of movement, breath, and mindfulness, understanding how this could reduce the inflammation and pain in her body. Over the weeks, it was a joy to witness her transformation as she moved from a state of feeling not in control of her body to one of empowerment, a testament to the strength of the subtlest of practices."

So, whether you stand in *tadasana* for ten minutes of quiet contemplation, or practice a steady sequence, in time this fresh, slow way of moving will have wonderful and long-lasting effects on body, mind, and soul.

STEADY AND STRONG

Experienced practitioners may choose to introduce the qualities of a steadier practice to their usual routine by, for example, taking a sun salutation back to basics. Move slowly from pose to pose, finding stillness and a sense of grounding and stability in each. Pause, taking five calm breaths and releasing a little deeper into the pose with each exhalation, before moving on.

Sun salutation (in Sanskrit *surya namaskar*) balances and energizes the body. It links body, breath, and mind and revitalizes both the physical and spiritual self. It also warms, strengthens, and aligns the entire body. You may do as many rounds as you wish.

- Stand tall, holding your hands, palms together, in prayer pose at your heart's center. Take a few deep breaths and focus on the self, your core, and your inner sun.

- Breathing in, circle your hands up above your head, reaching tall to the sun. Look up to the sky through your open arms, take five slow breaths.

- On an exhale, flow your arms down in a circle around your body to rest on the outside of each foot, with your fingers pointing forward in line with your toes. If needed, you can bend your knees slightly. Let your head hang toward the floor like a rag doll. Take five breaths here.

- On an inhale, straighten your legs and look forward. Step your left foot back into a lunge, staying here for five breaths.

- On an exhale, step your right foot back to join your left foot, forming a straight line with your body in plank pose—stay for five breaths.

- On an exhale, bend your knees and lower your body. Keep your knees on the floor and your elbows tucked in near the body. Take five deep breaths.

- Breathing in, push your chest upward into cobra pose (*bhujangasana*), opening your chest by drawing your shoulders back—take ten slow breaths here.

- On an exhale, tuck your toes under and push up into downward dog (*adho mukha savanasana*), pushing down into the floor through your hands and feet while your hips pull upward. Explore this posture in a mindful way, bringing full awareness to all sensations. Spend at least ten breaths here and either go deeper into it or explore the pose—you can rock your body weight from side to side, lift your legs, or shift your body weight from your hands to your feet and vice versa. Whatever feels good to you.

- On an inhale, step your right foot forward between your hands, forming a lunge position. Stay here for five breaths.

- Bring your left foot forward to join the right, forming a forward fold with your body. Stay here for thirty long, slow breaths, deepening the pose as much as is comfortable.

- Breathing in, slowly raise your hands and lift yourself to a standing tall position (your head comes up last). The hands join above the head in prayer position. Stay here for five breaths.

- Lower the hands to heart center and take a few deep breaths. Then repeat the sequence, this time taking your right leg back first for the initial lunge.

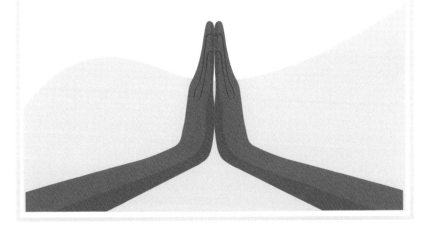

Dreams Do Come True

Rarely do dreams come stress-free, and sometimes there can be confusion, anxiety, doubt, or even disappointment after you've finally achieved a long-held ambition. However, being aware of this is the first step to help you move past these tricky emotions and find harmony.

Is there something you've dreamed of for a long time? It could be getting a book published, renovating your home, or taking early retirement. How do you imagine your life being better after this event? Reaching goals can feel rewarding, mood-boosting, and life-enhancing, but it can also be unsettling in some instances. Even positive change can threaten your sense of security and make you feel ungrounded. And, sometimes, it might not bring the happiness and fulfillment that you expected.

Major Life Changes

Betsey recently quit her job to pursue world travel. She says, "It's the sort of thing many people dream of doing, and I was no different. I spent over a year planning for my departure: saving money, selling my belongings, and renting out my house. The entire process was exciting, and I was thrilled for the real adventure to begin. Then a crazy thing happened. When I finally started traveling, I felt . . . strange.

"Suddenly new pressures existed that hadn't been there before—to make the most of my trip, to experience the unforgettable adventures that everyone associates with travel, and to make my trip into what other people expected it to be. The emotions were completely unexpected." Betsey also describes how traveling stripped her of her identity and made her question who she was.

Health Effects

For some, positive change can feel so stressful that it affects their health. This is what happened to journalist Kate Corney. "I got engaged, married, and had my first child in quick succession," she recalls. "[It was] a trio of happy things, but with them came rapid change and I experienced heart palpitations. It took a friend to see the root cause. It turns out even good change can take adjusting to."

Rethink the Changes

What can we do when seemingly positive change causes stress and isn't what we expected? Traveler Betsey began to focus on what she really wanted out of her trip and decided to think about what *she* wished to do rather than worry about how other people would perceive her adventures. New wife and mom Kate found the act of recognizing the stresses that had been brought by her happy life changes helped to alleviate her symptoms. At times of change—both positive and negative—it's easy to become stressed and lose connection with yourself. One thing to remember is to make allowances for the stress of positive change, be that moving house, moving in with a life partner, or landing a promotion at work.

Find Your Own Strategies

Debora Balardini, a Brazilian theater performer and director, has noticed she often experiences depression after the high of working on a production. "The mix of creativity, intensity, and living my dream as it unfolds with an incredibly talented ensemble during the conceptualization, preproduction, and production stages gives me a high for months," she says. "The job is highly collaborative and so intense that when the production, rehearsals, and shows are not there any more, the emptiness can feel tremendous."

Debora has developed her own strategies to cope with post-production lows. "I start preparing for the show's end a few weeks prior [to it happening]," she says. "I make sure my schedule has time for reflection, reading of new thought-provoking material, and plenty of time to rest. I try not to overstimulate myself with new things that are not priorities because the time to digest is crucial. I honor the feeling of longing as much as the excitement for the next new projects. As a creative with a background in hatha yoga, the practice of staying conscious, of being balanced, helps ensure that the feeling of longing doesn't consume my whole day."

Adrenaline Rush

If negative emotions and stress during times of positive change are troubling you, then this may be because the outcome is outside of your comfort zone. Helen Campbell, a career coach who works with creative freelancers and small business owners, says that when this happens the fight-or-flight response might kick in, causing an adrenaline rush and anxiety. Helen adds that change can also force you to examine how you think about yourself. "For example, someone might hold the belief that they're not confident. If this person is then shortlisted for an award, or invited to an event, they may start worrying about whether they have to make a speech or what they will wear instead of enjoying the recognition of being nominated."

Helen suggests that working with a coach is one way to get out of your comfort zone and embrace big changes. This is because it can help you to unlock what's going on under the surface and start to explore obstacles you feel might be in your way. Any change can bring unexpected feelings and outcomes, some of which will be welcomed, others not. If you're reaching for something you don't have it can be useful to bear in mind what's been taught for centuries by sages and spiritual teachers: real happiness is not about material possessions or external achievements. It comes from within.

EMBRACING POSITIVE CHANGE

Dealing with positive-change anxiety is the first step toward reaping your dream's benefits and finding balance.

1. Put It on Paper

Write down in advance all the positive aspects that will come from the change. Then, when you're surrounded by a sea of boxes in your new home and don't know where to start in unpacking them, or if you find the learning curve in your dream job is steeper than you imagined, referring to this list will give you the courage to persevere.

What will you gain from your major decision? Write down all the benefits to your life, however small, here.

....

....

....

....

....

....

....

....

....

....

....

....

....

....

GIVE YOURSELF A BREAK

When in the middle of your big change, check in with yourself and assess how you're feeling, as much as it's possible, every hour, on the hour.

You could try the following calming breathing technique:

- Breathe in for a count of four through your nose.

- Pause briefly, then breathe out through your nose for a count of eight.

- As you exhale, focus on releasing unnecessary nervous tension and repeat a mantra to yourself such as "all is well" or "I'm in control." Over time, these affirmative statements could help you feel better able to cope.

2. Reevaluate Your Goals

Whatever your goals or dreams, it's important to ask yourself what brings happiness. Although success can give a sense of fulfillment, it's difficult to feel great when you're so busy you lose sight of the present moment. Even if you're striving for lofty goals, the rules of practicing self-care still apply.

When do you feel happy? When have you felt the most happiness in the past? Are there any unexpected harbingers of joy? Write down your responses and reflect on what the common thread of these might be.

....

....

....

....

....

....

....

....

....

....

....

....

....

....

....

....

....

....

Bringing awareness to these moments can highlight that happiness often occurs when you feel a sense of well-being in body and mind. It can be useful to anticipate and prepare for some of the trickier feelings that may flow after completing a goal.

STERLING
New York

An Imprint of Sterling Publishing Co., Inc.

STERLING and the distinctive Sterling logo are registered trademarks of
Sterling Publishing Co., Inc.

ISBN 978-1-4549-4399-0

Distributed in Canada by Sterling Publishing Co., Inc.
c/o Canadian Manda Group, 664 Annette Street
Toronto, Ontario M6S 2C8, Canada

For information about custom editions, special sales, and premium and corporate
purchases, please contact Sterling Special Sales at 800-805-5489 or
specialsales@sterlingpublishing.com.

Manufactured in Singapore

2 4 6 8 10 9 7 5 3 1

sterlingpublishing.com

Editorial: Susie Duff, Samita Foria, Catherine Kielthy, Jane Roe
Design: Jo Chapman
Publisher: Jonathan Grogan

Words credits: Dawattie Basdeo, Jenny Cockle, Beverley D'Silva, Karen Edwards,
Juliana Kassianos, Chloe Menage, Kate Orson, Caroline Pattenden, Kate Schuyler,
Simone Scott, Kat Smith, Gabrielle Treanor

Illustrations: Louise Billyard, Rialda Dizdarevic, Weronika Kuc, Amy Leonard, Jianan Liu,
Irina Perju, Silvia Stecher, Kate Styling, Sirin Thada, Sara Thielker
Cover illustration: Agnesbic